What Are the Ten Commandments?

by Yona Zeldis McDonough

illustrated by Tim Foley

Penguin Workshop

For my mother, Malcah Zeldis—YZM

PENGUIN WORKSHOP
An Imprint of Penguin Random House LLC, New York

The publisher does not have any control over and does not assume any responsibility for author or third-party websites or their content.

Copyright © 2017 by Penguin Random House LLC. All rights reserved. Published by Penguin Workshop, an imprint of Penguin Random House LLC, New York. PENGUIN and PENGUIN WORKSHOP are trademarks of Penguin Books Ltd. WHO HQ & Design is a registered trademark of Penguin Random House LLC. Printed in the USA.

Visit us online at www.penguinrandomhouse.com.

Library of Congress Control Number: 2017032507

ISBN 9780515157239 (paperback)   10 9 8 7 6 5 4 3
ISBN 9780515157253 (library binding)   10 9 8 7 6 5 4 3 2 1

Contents

What Are the Ten Commandments?

c. 1446 BC

According to the Old Testament of the Bible, for three long months, Moses led his people, the ancient Israelites, as they escaped from Egypt into the desert. The land was parched and dry. The sun was scorching. The journey was long. But everyone believed God would protect them and lead them to the Promised Land. Finally, they came to Mount Sinai and pitched their tents—600,000 men, as well as women and children.

Leaving his followers, Moses went up Mount Sinai, where he heard God's words. God said that if the children of Israel obeyed His laws, He would make them His Chosen People—special in His eyes. God also said He had a gift for them. He would give it to Moses in three days.

Moses shared this news with the Israelites. He told them to begin praying because God had promised to appear again to Moses very soon. The Israelites spent the next three days in prayer. On the third day, a thick cloud appeared above the mountain. That was not all. There were claps of thunder and bolts of lightning. There was also the loud, powerful sound of a trumpet.

God called Moses to the mountaintop again, to receive the gift: It was a pair of large stone tablets. On them were carved ten rules for leading a good life and loving God. They were the Ten Commandments, which the Bible says are the only laws written "by the finger of God." And they are as important today as they were so long ago, in Moses's time.

Who Were the Israelites?

The Israelites, or Hebrews, were an ancient Jewish people who came from different tribes. According to the Bible, the tribes were descended from the sons and grandsons of their Jewish ancestor, Jacob. They are called Israelites because Israel was the name God gave to Jacob. The names of the tribes are Reuben, Simeon, Judah, Issachar, Zebulun, Dan, Naphtali, Gad, Asher, Ephraim, Benjamin, and Manasseh. Levi, another son of Jacob, founded a priestly tribe that was considered distinct from the other twelve tribes.

Jacob

CHAPTER 1
The Israelites Become Slaves

c. 1526 BC

For many years, the Israelites had lived and thrived in the ancient kingdom of Egypt. They were different from their neighbors. Unlike the Egyptians, the Israelites believed in one almighty God. And no other. The Egyptians believed in many gods.

The Israelites in Egypt had descended from Joseph, a son of Jacob, and his family. Joseph's brothers had sold him into slavery there. Though Joseph began as a slave, he became a powerful man in Egypt. He was an adviser to the pharaoh (king). He had many children and grandchildren. Joseph's father's family joined him

Joseph

in Egypt, and they too had many children. Over the years, there came to be many Israelites in Egypt—hundreds of thousands.

Much later on, the pharaoh ruling over Egypt began to fear the Israelites. What if they rebelled against him? Or even worse—what if they left Egypt? So Pharaoh decided to enslave the Israelites.

The Great Pyramids at Giza

Did the Jewish slaves in Egypt build the pyramids at Giza? There are many stories that say so. But the Great Pyramids had already been built about a thousand years earlier. The Great Pyramids were completed around 2500 BC. So the story is not true. Jewish slaves could not have built them. Egyptian laborers did.

From then on, the Israelites were mistreated and abused. They had to work long and hard for the pharaoh, building cities for him. But did hard labor kill off the Israelites, as the pharaoh had hoped?

No. It did not.

This made the pharaoh even angrier. So he gave a command. Every newborn Israelite boy was to be thrown into the Nile River and drowned. He would let the baby girls live because when they grew up, there would be no men for them to marry. There would be no Israelite babies born. The Israelites whom Pharaoh hated and feared would die out.

Around this time, an Israelite couple named Amram (say: AM-ram) and Jochebed (say: YAH-keh-bed) had a baby boy. They already had a daughter, Miriam, and a son named Aaron. Somehow they had kept Aaron safe from the Egyptians. But how could they keep their newborn safe? A crying baby was sure to be discovered.

Jochebed loved her infant son and could not bear the thought of him being drowned. So she put him in a small basket and set it floating on the Nile River. Then she hid behind the bulrushes that grew at the water's edge and waited. She prayed that someone would find her baby and take good care of him. Her daughter, Miriam, was beside her.

The Bible goes on to tell how Pharaoh's daughter, the princess, soon came down to the river to bathe. Her servants were with her. The princess saw the basket and sent a maid to get it.

In the basket was a crying baby boy!

The princess was sure the baby must belong to an Israelite couple who had refused to drown their child. The princess felt pity for him, a little baby alone on the river. The princess decided she would keep the baby safe.

At that moment, the baby's sister came out of hiding. Miriam asked if the princess needed a family to care for the baby. The princess said yes. So Miriam took the princess to Jochebed. Pharaoh's daughter told Jochebed to look after the baby for a while. Later on the boy would be brought to Pharaoh's court. After that, the princess would raise the boy as her own child. He would be a prince of Egypt.

Without knowing it, the princess had asked the baby's very own mother to raise him.

CHAPTER 2
An Egyptian Prince

Jochebed cared for the baby and did everything Pharaoh's daughter had asked. When her son was a little boy, she brought him to live with the royal family.

The princess named the boy Moses. It means *drawn out*, because he had been drawn out of the river Nile. From then on, Moses grew up surrounded by the luxury of Pharaoh's court.

The princess told her father she had adopted the child. Her father did not object, even though Pharaoh knew the boy must be an Israelite. Why didn't Pharaoh object? It was because Pharaoh believed in astrology.

An astrologer tries to predict the future by looking at the position of different stars. Pharaoh's astrologer told him that someone had been marked to set the Israelites free. But this person had already been drowned. So Pharaoh had nothing to fear from little Moses.

When Moses was a young man, he saw an Egyptian slave master whipping an Israelite—one of his own people. Making sure none of Pharaoh's men were watching, Moses killed the Egyptian and hid his body in the sand.

Even so, Pharaoh learned about the murder and wanted Moses put to death. Moses had to flee. He escaped to the land of Midian (say: MID-ee-an). Midian was a good distance from the Nile in Egypt, and Moses would be safe there.

In Midian, Moses married Zipporah (say: ZIP-er-ah), an Israelite and the daughter of a shepherd. They had a son named Gershom, which means "stranger."

Zipporah

Moses chose that name because he, too, felt like a stranger in a new land. Moses lived in Midian for forty years.

How Did Moses Know He Was an Israelite?

Are you wondering about this? Well, this question has puzzled people for a long time. There is no explanation given in the Bible. But perhaps Jochebed told her son about his heritage before he left to live with Pharaoh's daughter in the Egyptian court. Or maybe he saw that he looked like other Israelites. There are many unanswered questions in the story of Moses.

By this time, the pharaoh who had condemned Moses had died. There was a new pharaoh. But he was no friend to the Israelites, either. Under his rule, they remained slaves.

The Bible says that one day when Moses was in the desert tending his father-in-law's flock of sheep, he saw a remarkable sight: a bush was on fire. Though the bush burned, it was not destroyed by the flames. Then something even more miraculous happened.

A voice began speaking to Moses from inside the bush! It was God.

God told him that He had seen the misery of the Israelites, and that He wanted them to be free. Moses was the man He had chosen to lead everyone from slavery to freedom in Canaan—the Promised Land.

Moses was astounded. Why was he the one God had chosen for this enormous task? He wasn't a powerful king. He was just a shepherd.

God told Moses to return to Egypt and gather the enslaved Israelites. Moses was to beg the new pharaoh to allow the Israelites to leave for the desert. If Pharaoh said yes, the Israelites would spend three days worshipping God. The one almighty God.

God was sure the king of Egypt would not let this happen. And so God was going to prove His power to Pharaoh through certain signs. He asked Moses to hit his shepherd's rod on the ground. The rod turned into a snake, then returned to its original form once Moses picked it up.

Next, God had Moses place his hand to his chest. When he removed it, his hand was white and withered. Again he put his hand against his chest, and it became normal. Moses would show these signs to Pharaoh.

Moses returned to Egypt with his family and his brother, Aaron. Moses and Aaron went to Pharaoh and repeated God's words, to set the Israelites free.

Pharaoh, however, didn't believe in the God of the Israelites and refused. He sent Moses and Aaron away. He was angry that they had dared to come before him. He told the slave masters to make the Israelites work even harder.

The Israelites needed straw to make bricks for the buildings they were forced to construct. However, from now on, no straw would be given to them. The Israelites would have to gather the straw for themselves. This would take time—and

yet they still had to make as many bricks as they had before.

Now the slaves were even worse off. The Israelites blamed Moses and Aaron.

The Bible says that once again God told Moses to return to Pharaoh and say that the Israelites had to be set free. He did, and he demonstrated God's power by having Aaron cast his staff on the ground, where it turned into a snake. The Egyptians were not impressed. Pharaoh's magicians did the same with their own staffs. But Aaron's serpent ate theirs. Even so, the king would not listen.

This time, by the Nile River, Moses showed Pharaoh another sign from God. Moses handed his rod to Aaron. Aaron struck the water.

What happened next? The Bible says that the water turned to blood. The river smelled terrible. All the fish died.

The Egyptians were afraid to drink from it or to use it to bathe. But Pharaoh still refused to listen, so God sent another plague. (A plague means a disaster.) This time, when Aaron struck the river, thousands of frogs jumped from its banks. They swarmed Egypt, entering every corner of every house. Pharaoh was frightened now. He told Moses if he got rid of the frogs, the Israelites could leave Egypt.

Moses prayed, and God made the frogs die. But when the plague had ended, Pharaoh changed his mind. So God sent another plague, this time lice.

The bugs infested the animals and the Egyptians. Every man, woman, child, and beast tried in vain to scratch, scratch, scratch away the terrible itch.

Next came horrible, dirty flies that swarmed everywhere.

Seeing this, Pharaoh agreed to let the Israelites leave for the desert. Again Moses prayed that the plague be lifted, and the flies disappeared.

And once more, Pharaoh took back his word. He did not let the Israelites go.

God sent more plagues: all the cattle in Egypt died. The Egyptians became covered in sores. There was a huge hailstorm. Locusts invaded  their fields, eating away every last growing thing. There were three solid days of darkness during which the sun did not rise. Over and over, Pharaoh promised to let the slaves go. And each time, he broke his promise. He still did not believe in the power of God.

Finally, Moses told Pharaoh about the tenth plague God would deliver. It was the worst by far. All the firstborn sons in Egypt would die. But the Israelite children would be spared.

That night, Moses told his people to smear lamb's blood on the doorways of their houses. God would see the lamb's blood. He would know it was a sign that the people inside were Israelites. He would pass over their houses. Their children would be safe.

Soon Pharaoh heard the sound of weeping coming from homes where there was a death. The death of every firstborn male child. Even Pharaoh's own son died. Finally convinced of God's power,

Pharaoh let the Israelites go. Moses could lead his people out of slavery. After four hundred years as slaves, the Israelites were finally free.

Passover

Passover is one of the most important Jewish holidays. On Passover, Jews around the world remember the time when God "passed over" the homes of the Israelites but killed all the firstborn sons of the Egyptians. Passover also celebrates the story of the Israelite slaves' freedom. Passover goes on for eight days. Every year, Jews retell the story of their slavery and their freedom. This telling takes place during the seder (say: SAY-der), a service held at home on the first night and sometimes the second night, too. Jews read the story aloud from a book called a Haggadah (say: ha-GAH-dah). They eat special foods like the large flat crackers called matzo to help them remember the story. (The Israelites had to flee from Egypt so quickly, they didn't have time to put yeast in the bread they were baking, so it did not rise—it stayed flat.)

CHAPTER 3
Into the Desert

The story in the Bible continues with the Israelites heading east on foot. God guided them as they went. Still, their troubles were not over.

Right away, Pharaoh was angry over what he'd done. He sent his army to capture the Israelites.

Camping by the Sea of Reeds, the Israelites saw Egyptian soldiers marching toward them. (Today, no one knows for sure where the Sea of Reeds was.) They saw their mighty chariots. They saw their horses. Frightened and bitter, the Israelites asked Moses if they had escaped from slavery only to be killed in the wilderness.

Moses turned to God, who said that the Israelites had to keep going forward. He would

keep them safe. If Moses lifted up his rod while stretching his hand over the sea, the sea would part. The children of Israel would pass through the middle of the sea unharmed. So Moses did just what God said. He stretched out his hand, and a strong wind blew all night. The sea parted. A wall of water rose up on either side, letting the Israelites walk through.

The Egyptians were not far behind. However, once they reached the sea, the wheels of their chariots got stuck in the mud. As soon as the Israelites had crossed, God told Moses to stretch his hand over the waters again. He did, and the walls of water broke, crashing down on the Egyptians. They all drowned.

God had saved the Israelites.

For almost three months, the Israelites traveled through the desert. Finally, they came to Mount Sinai. It was there that God gave Moses the precious gift of the Ten Commandments.

For forty days and forty nights, he stayed listening to God. God gave Moses other laws about not destroying others' property, the right way to treat people, and how to celebrate the Sabbath and other holidays.

The Sabbath

The Sabbath is a day each week that is set aside for rest and worship. According to the Book of Exodus in the Bible, God commanded the Sabbath to be kept as a holy day of rest. Just as God rested from creating the world on the seventh day, people were supposed to take a break from work and many daily activities. For Jews, the Sabbath lasts from sundown on Friday when candles are lit to sundown on Saturday. Most Christians observe the Sabbath on Sundays. Although Muslims generally do not celebrate Sabbath the way Jews and Christians do, Friday is a special day of prayer in Islam.

In addition, God told Moses to build a special chest called an ark to carry the tablets of the Ten Commandments. It would travel under a tent called a tabernacle because no one was supposed to look at the ark—it was too holy. The Israelites were supposed to make offerings of grain and animal sacrifices to God at the tabernacle.

CHAPTER 4
Forty Years of Wandering

During the forty days and nights that Moses spent listening to God on Mount Sinai, the Israelites grew worried. They thought Moses might be dead. If so, what would happen to them? Who would be their leader? They went to Aaron and said they needed a new god to worship. The first of the Ten Commandments said this was wrong. Still, Aaron told them to bring him all their gold jewelry and trinkets. He then melted them down and made an idol (a statue) of a golden calf. He showed the calf to the Israelites. He told them the calf was now their god.

The next day, the people woke up early. They brought offerings to the calf, like burned meat. They had a feast. They danced and sang.

God saw what they were doing. He was furious. How quickly they had forgotten His commandments! They were to worship Him and only Him. He was so angry, He wanted to destroy all the Israelites. But Moses begged for mercy. And God listened.

Moses went down the mountain. He carried the two stone tablets on which the commandments were written. When he saw his people dancing

around the golden calf, he was very angry. He threw the tablets down at the foot of the mountain. The tablets broke into pieces. Then he took the golden calf and burned it.

What was left, he ground into powder. He tossed the powder on the water and made the Israelites drink it. Then Moses wrote the commandments on a new set of tablets. And he killed the Israelites who still wanted to worship the golden calf.

Moses made a promise to God. The Israelites would obey His laws, and He would be their God. In return, the Israelites would reach the Promised Land.

The Promised Land

According to the Bible, the Promised Land—the land of Canaan (say: KAY-nan)—was given to the Israelites by God. It would be their home if they obeyed God's word. They could build a nation there. The Promised Land was said in the Book of Genesis to be the territory from the River of Egypt to the Euphrates River. Later, it was narrowed down to a smaller area of Canaan. Today, most Jews believe that the present-day nation of Israel fulfills God's ancient promise.

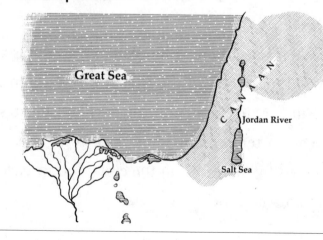

Moses led the faithful Israelites to the Desert of Paran, near Canaan. They were still searching for the Promised Land. He sent twelve men into Canaan. They came back saying the land was good for growing crops. But they also said the people who lived there were giants.

Hearing that, some of the Israelites wanted to go back to Egypt. Some rebelled against Moses. Moses told the Israelites that they did not deserve the Promised Land. They would have to wander in the desert for forty years until everyone who refused to enter Canaan had died. Then their children could go to their new home.

When forty more years passed, Moses was a very old man. He led the Israelites east around the Salt Sea, to Edom and Moab. The Israelites were again tempted by idols, and were harshly punished by God. But in the end, God forgave them and gave them His blessing. After singing a song of praise to God, Moses went up to the top of Mount Nebo alone. He gazed over at the Promised Land. Then he died.

Moses had led the Israelites out of Egypt, but he never reached the Promised Land himself. According to the Bible, this is how God meant it to be.

CHAPTER 5
After Moses

With Moses gone, who would become the leader of the Israelites? Who would take them to the Promised Land?

It was Joshua. He had become very close to Moses and took his place. Joshua is considered one of the great leaders of Jewish history.

When Joshua took charge, the Israelites were still east of the Jordan River. God had promised to give them the land west of the Jordan. But many different peoples were living there—groups of Canaanites, Hittites, and others. These people had built cities that were protected by strong armies. Would they just give up their homes when the Israelites came?

Not likely.

Ancient Canaanite city

Before entering the new land, the Israelites sent a messenger to the Canaanites. The message said that God, the Creator of the Universe, had promised the land to them. They were now ready to claim it and wanted the Canaanites to leave peacefully. But only a few Canaanites left. So what happened next?

The Israelites crossed the Jordan—God parted the waters for them as He had done before when they escaped from Egypt. Carrying the Ark of the Covenant, the Israelites set up camp before beginning a series of attacks.

The first battle was fought at Jericho. This city was at the entrance to the heartland of Canaan. Jericho was protected by walls all around. Yet the Israelites won easily, with the walls of Jericho falling before their amazed eyes. (Some archaeologists have suggested that a well-timed earthquake caused the walls to fall.)

Then the Israelites moved on to the next city-state, called Ai. But unlike the battle of Jericho, the fighting did not go well. The Israelites met with a terrible defeat. Many were killed.

Why had they lost? they wondered. Had God abandoned them? After all, He had promised them this land.

They soon learned that at Jericho one of the Israelites had taken treasure for himself. This was against one of God's commandments. It was stealing. And so, because one person had disobeyed God's laws, all the Israelites had to suffer.

After that they went on to conquer Ai and many other places, including the city of Jerusalem, where a people called Jebusites lived. (Long after, Jerusalem became the capital city of the Kingdom of Israel and was where King Solomon built a great and famous temple.)

Despite other hardships, the Israelites took over the Promised Land. It was bordered by Egypt to the south and Mesopotamia to the north. After twenty-eight years, Joshua died and some of the Israelites fell back to worshipping idols. Again they suffered God's anger. But not all the Israelites broke this holy commandment. There were enough Israelites who still obeyed God's rule, and so the roots of a Jewish nation kept growing.

Jerusalem Today

Jerusalem is now the lively, bustling capital city of Israel, the world's only Jewish nation. It is also an important religious center, considered holy not only to Jews but also to Christians and Muslims. People of all three faiths worship at the city's temples, churches, and mosques.

Abbey of the Dormition

Muslims living in Jerusalem and Israel call themselves Palestinians. Some Palestinians believe they are descended from the Canaanites, the ancient residents of area, and have declared their own country: Palestine. Israelis say the Promised Land belongs to them. Israel controls Palestine.

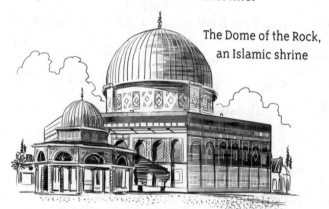

The Dome of the Rock, an Islamic shrine

Until 1967, East Jerusalem was under Muslim control, with West Jerusalem under Israeli control. Today, Israel controls all of Jerusalem, but Palestinians claim East Jerusalem as their capital. Some nations recognize Palestine as its own country; the United States does not.

CHAPTER 6
One God vs. Many Gods

In the Ten Commandments, God says that He must be worshipped as the one and only god. Yet in the story of Moses, the Israelites disobeyed this commandment more than once. Perhaps this was because in ancient times, belief in one almighty God was unusual.

Many civilizations were polytheistic. That means they worshipped lots of different gods and goddesses. (*Poly* means *many*, and *theo* means *god*.) In the part of the world that covers much of what is known as the Middle East, ancient Canaanites, Phoenicians, Hittites, Assyrians, and Babylonians all had polytheistic religions. So did the ancient Greeks and Romans of southern Europe. People of these religions often worshipped statues of their gods. Worshippers made sacrifices to them. They asked for favors. They hoped the gods would grant their wishes.

The ancient Egyptians who lived in the time of Moses believed in a group of gods and goddesses who were in control of nature, life, and death. The Egyptians created myths, or stories, about these gods to explain their powers.

Temple at Karnak in Egypt

The pharaoh was also important in Egyptian religion. Although he was a human, the Egyptians believed he was descended from the gods. He was a link between those gods and his people. That made him special, because ordinary people could not communicate with the important gods and goddesses. Only Pharaoh could.

A pharaoh with the god Anubis

Egyptians believed in an afterlife. It was very much like everyday life on earth. So tombs were built for the dead and filled with all the objects—food, games, furniture—the dead person would need to enjoy the afterlife. The tombs of the pharaohs held astounding treasures.

King Tut's tomb

Egyptian Gods and Goddesses

Here are some of the important Egyptian gods and goddesses. Many looked like humans except for their heads, which were often in the shape of an animal's head.

Osiris

Osiris, god of agriculture and ruler of the dead. He was shown with the head of a bird, probably a falcon.

Isis, wife of Osiris, mother of Horus and Mistress of Magic. She was sometimes shown with the horns and ears of a cow.

Horus, son of Osiris, a sky god. Like his father, he was often shown with the head of a falcon.

Set, enemy of Horus and Osiris, god of storms and disorder. He was shown with the head of a doglike beast.

Thoth, a moon deity and god of writing, counting, and wisdom. Thoth was sometimes shown with the body of a baboon and the head of a dog.

Hathor, goddess of love, birth, and death. Like Isis, she was sometimes shown with the ears and horns of a cow.

Anubis, god of mummification (preserving the bodies of the dead). He was shown with the head of a jackal.

Ra, the sun god. He was shown with the head of a bird that is most likely a heron.

Amun, a creator god; sometimes identified with Ra, but often depicted with the head of a ram.

Anubis

Aten, a sun god, also sometimes identified with Ra, often shown with the head of a falcon.

The religion of the ancient Egyptians lasted for roughly three thousand years. For a short time, when one pharaoh named Akhenaten was in power, he told his people to worship only Aten—the sun god. Some historians who study different religions see this change as being similar to the Israelites worshipping one God. But other historians do not. This new Egyptian religion lasted only for a little while. After Akhenaten was dead, the Egyptians went back to their practice of worshipping many gods again.

Akhenaten

The Israelites were different from other ancient peoples. They were monotheistic. That means their religion was based on the belief in one and only one almighty God.

One God?

In modern times, have all religions become monotheistic?

No. There are many religions that include multiple gods, like Hinduism. Krishna, Shiva, Vishnu, Shakti, Ganesha (the elephant god), and Surya (the sun god) are a few of the gods worshipped in the Hindu faith.

Ganesha

Shiva

Krishna

CHAPTER 7
The Commandments, One by One

The Ten Commandments together form the foundation of both Judaism and Christianity. They are first and foremost a set of laws. They are often referred to as the Decalogue (say: DECK-a-log), a word that means *ten words*, as in ten words of God. Today, both Jews and Christians follow these commandments, though the wording and the order may vary.

They can be broken down in these ways:

Commandments One, Two, and Three are about God. He identifies Himself. He forbids the worship of idols. And He forbids using His name in any way that doesn't respect Him.

Commandments Four and Five tell people the proper way to behave. They must always remember to observe the Sabbath and honor their parents.

Commandments Six through Nine tell people what they must never do. They forbid murder, being disloyal through adultery, stealing from others, and accusing people of a crime they didn't commit.

Commandment Ten is about not envying what other people have.

By looking at the commandments separately and more closely, a clearer sense comes through of what each one means.

First Commandment *I am the Lord, your God. You shall have no other gods before me.*

This is really more of a statement than a commandment. It is so important because it is about faith and loyalty. God demands that His followers worship only Him. And it establishes the Israelites, later known as the Jews, as the followers of a religion that was very different from any other at the time.

Moses burning the golden calf

Second Commandment *You shall not make for yourself a graven image; you shall not bow down to them and worship them.*

Many religions prayed to or worshipped "graven images," which meant statues. It was believed they had divine powers. This commandment says to give up the worship of such false objects. Instead, people must pray to God directly.

Third Commandment *You shall not take the name of the Lord your God in vain.*

This means no one should swear using God's name. But also it means something else. No one should use God as an excuse for committing bad or selfish acts.

When a person does something bad, he discredits—or brings shame on—himself. But if he does something bad in the name of God, that discredits God. Since God relies on His followers to bring His truth to the world, He considers this a sin.

Fourth Commandment *Remember the Sabbath day, to keep it holy.*

This commandment is about showing respect for God by setting aside a special day every week to honor Him. God did not want people to work on the Sabbath. They were supposed to pray and think about Him. But this commandment has another purpose. In ancient times, people worked very hard, often seven days a week. A commandment about the Sabbath shows God's kindness and mercy toward people. Everyone needs a day of rest.

Fifth Commandment *Honor your father and mother.*

The first four commandments are about people and God. This is the first commandment about how people should treat one another. It reminds us that it is most important to always show respect for our parents who gave us life and to care for them when they are old.

Sixth Commandment *You shall not murder.*

This commandment forbids killing anyone in cold blood. That means you cannot harm somebody just because you are angry at them. However, it does not forbid killing in times of war or self-defense—if an enemy is trying to kill you. But to kill out of anger, or for any other personal reason, is forbidden.

Seventh Commandment *You shall not commit adultery.*

When people get married, they promise to love only one person—the person they marry.

Yet sometimes people break this promise and fall in love with someone else. This commandment tells married couples that they must stay true to each other.

Eighth Commandment *You shall not steal.*

This commandment helps society run smoothly. It sets out a clear rule about not taking what does not belong to you. And it

protects your belongings from being taken by someone else.

Ninth Commandment *You shall not bear false witness against your neighbor.*

This commandment is about telling the truth. It says that it is wrong to accuse someone of something they have not done.

Tenth Commandment *You shall not covet your neighbor's house . . . or anything else that belongs to your neighbor.*

This commandment is different from the three that came before it. The tenth commandment is not about simply behaving properly; it goes deeper than that. It has to do with feelings of envy and jealousy. It's easy to want what other people have, whether it's a big house, a fancy car, or a private jet. But the commandment reminds us to be happy with what we have, and not spend time comparing ourselves to others. It also helps us to keep the other commandments faithfully.

CHAPTER 8
Was Moses Real?

The story of how Moses received God's Ten Commandments is told in the Book of Exodus in the Old Testament of the Bible. *Exodus* means *leaving*, and that is what Moses and the Israelites did. They left Egypt for God's Promised Land.

The commandments are listed again in the Book of Deuteronomy. Both accounts say that God inscribed them on two stone tablets that He gave to Moses. In the New Testament, they are mentioned again in Mark 7:10 and John 7:19.

Certainly many people, both Jewish and Christian, believe that all the stories in the Bible happened exactly as they are told. For instance, they believe that God created the world in six days as described in the Book of Genesis. Other people do not believe the stories word for word but still believe in God. They respect and obey the teachings in the Bible. It offers them a guide to living a good life. So there are different ways to believe in the Bible.

As for Moses and the story of the Ten Commandments, how factual is it? Did it happen in exactly the way the Bible says? For some, there are many questions that do not have clear answers. Some historians who study religion are not even sure Moses was a real person.

Why?

There are parts of his story that seem to contradict—or go against—each other. The Bible appears to give different facts in different places. In one part of the Bible, it seems as if Moses is an only child. Later, however, his older sister Miriam and older brother Aaron come into the story.

The Bible

The Old Testament is the first part of the Bible. The New Testament is the second part. Jewish people read only the Old Testament. The first five books of the Old Testament, sometimes called the Torah, are:

Genesis—Tells the stories of the creation of the world, the fall of Adam and Eve, Noah's ark and the Flood, as well as the stories of Abraham, Isaac, Jacob, and Joseph.

Exodus—Tells the stories of Moses, the ten plagues that God sent, Passover, the escape from Egypt, crossing the Sea of Reeds, and God's gift of the Ten Commandments on Mount Sinai.

Leviticus—Gives lessons on the priesthood, and on the laws of cleanliness, which are called kashrut or kosher.

Numbers—Tells the stories of the golden calf and the start of the forty years in the desert.

Deuteronomy—Repeats the laws of God, like the Ten Commandments and holy days. Blessings are promised to those who obey the law, and famine is promised to those who break it.

The New Testament goes on to tell about the life, death, and resurrection (coming to life again) of Jesus. For Christians, Jesus is the son of God and the savior of mankind.

Also, things are left out of the Bible that seem puzzling. Exodus tells how Moses was adopted by an Egyptian princess, but then nothing is written about his childhood with the pharaoh. And the only account of Moses's death is vague. No one knows where he is buried. These missing pieces make some people doubt his existence.

Here is something else to think about: The ancient Egyptians were known for keeping careful records of almost everything. Yet there is no mention anywhere of the Israelites leaving the country. Why was nothing written down about such a major event?

Egyptian scribe

Also, the Exodus story tells of the Israelites—a very huge number of them—wandering through a certain area of desert for years and years. Archaeologists are scientists who look for objects from the past to learn about people who lived in an area long ago. The desert around Mount Sinai has been searched in the hope of turning up evidence to prove the ancient Israelites were there. So far none has been found. The ark and the tablets that the Israelites carried with them to the Promised Land have never been found, either.

These are questions that continue to interest scholars and historians. But the Bible stories about Moses are very powerful. Many people will continue to believe them. Many take them word for word. Each person is free to decide how much of the story she or he believes and what it means to them.

CHAPTER 9
The Covenant with God

The Bible says that about a year after fleeing from Egypt, Moses directed the Israelites to build the Ark of the Covenant. This was a wooden chest covered in gold. Along with other holy texts, the ark contained the two stone tablets with the Ten Commandments. Since Moses broke the first tablets, it is believed that he wrote down another set. Those would be the tablets in the Ark of the Covenant.

What is a covenant?

It is an agreement. Like a contract.

In a contract, each side agrees to do something, and in return, each side gets something back. The Israelites made a contract or covenant with God. By following the Ten Commandments

and believing in His word, the Israelites would become God's Chosen People. He would look out for them, lead them to the Promised Land, and help them in times of hardship.

What Do the Names and Numbers in the Bible Mean?

The Ten Commandments are first mentioned in the Bible in Exodus 20:1–17. The names and numbers are put there to help readers find a section easily. They break down into three distinct parts: book, chapter, and verse.

The book name tells us which book in the Bible we need to be looking for. If you don't know the order of the Bible that well, you can find the different books listed in the front.

Next, there is a chapter number. This helps find the rough location of the passage within the book. The chapter number is printed in large bold type, making it easy to see.

The final number (or numbers) point to a particular verse (or verses) in the chapter. Each chapter has small numbers that appear throughout the text. These are the verse numbers and allow you to find exactly the lines you are looking for.

While the Bible was always broken up into books, the books were not divided into chapters and verses for a long time. Modern chapter divisions were made in the thirteenth century, and verses in the sixteenth century.

The words of the Ten Commandments were carved into stone tablets. The translation of the Hebrew phrase for making a covenant is *cutting a covenant*. That's because in ancient times, signing an agreement was often marked with an animal sacrifice, so the "cutting" was for real.

The Ten Commandments were placed in a very special place—the Ark of the Covenant. This is similar to the way important documents, like contracts, are now kept in a safe-deposit box at the bank. It keeps them protected.

A modern-day rabbi holding a Torah with an ark behind him

Also, in ancient times, contracts or treaties would sometimes be read aloud publicly at regular times. This is true of the commandments, which the Bible says are to be read aloud "every seven years . . . before all men, women, and children" (Deuteronomy 31:10–12). During the period of the great Second Temple in Jerusalem, the Ten Commandments were recited daily. In later centuries, rabbis (teachers or priests of the Jewish religion) stopped this practice. They worried that people would mistakenly think that they only had to obey the Ten Commandments.

In fact, in the Bible, there are listed many more commandments than the ten given to Moses on Mount Sinai. The first five books of the Old Testament contain at least 613 commandments. Many are about how people should worship. There are commandments about helping people who are in danger, giving charity to the poor, and respecting both neighbors and strangers. The list also includes laws about everyday life—such things as ownership of property and rules for who can testify in court. But the Ten Commandments are understood to be the most important laws. Taken together, they outline a contract showing how to honor God, ourselves, and the people around us.

The places where Jewish people come to pray are called temples or synagogues. Today, the Ten Commandments are heard in synagogues three times a year. They are read when they come up in the regular reading of the Bible, and also during a holiday known as the Festival of Weeks, called Shavuot (say: shuh-VOO-ut). Shavuot celebrates the grain harvest. In some traditions, worshippers rise for the reading of the Ten Commandments to show respect for their special importance.

The Second Temple

The Second Temple was an important Jewish Holy Temple that stood on the Temple Mount in Jerusalem between 515 BC and AD 70. According to Jewish tradition, it replaced the first temple (called Solomon's Temple) that was destroyed in 586 BC when the Babylonians conquered Jerusalem.

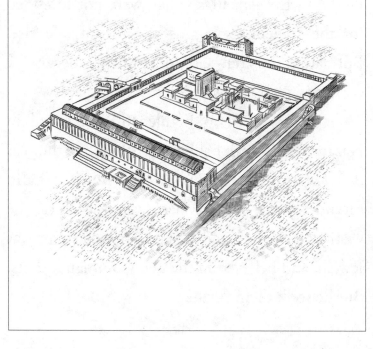

CHAPTER 10
The Commandments and Other Religions

When the Ten Commandments were first written down, they were not meant to apply to all people. Instead, they were a contract only between God and the Israelites. They were not intended for the ancient Egyptians—or for anyone else. But later, the Ten Commandments became a cornerstone of a new religion—Christianity.

Jesus was born in Bethlehem and raised in Nazareth. His birth has been attributed to the year AD 1. (AD means *anno domini*, which is Latin for *year of our lord*.) When Jesus was thirty, he went to Jerusalem and began to preach. Jesus was Jewish, and believed in the Ten Commandments. But he took them further.

Many people began to listen to Jesus. They called him a king. They even said he was the son of God. The Jews of the time considered this blasphemy, and many were furious with Jesus and his followers. The Romans did not like this, either. They feared his power would challenge theirs, and they killed him in AD 33. But Jesus's followers said that three days later, Jesus came back to life, and remained with them until he went to rejoin God in heaven.

Jesus's teachings became a new religion: Christianity. At first, the Christians were a small group and were persecuted by the Romans. But finally, in AD 312, the Roman emperor Constantine decreed that it was no longer a crime to be a Christian. And he officially converted to

Emperor Constantine

Christianity before his death in the year 337.

Christians believe in the divine authority of the Ten Commandments. They consider them a summary of God's law and a standard of good behavior. The commandments are at the core of Christian life and worship.

One of the biggest differences between Christianity and Judaism is that Christians believe Jesus is the son of God. Jews do not. Judaism sees Jesus as being a great prophet or teacher. Like Moses.

During his life, Jesus talked often about the Ten Commandments. He also added another "commandment" to the list: Thou shalt love thy neighbor as thyself. This is often called the Golden Rule.

Jesus delivered his Sermon on the Mount, a collection of moral teachings, on Mount Eremos. The Sermon is the longest speech from Jesus in the New Testament, and it contains the

most well-known of the teachings Jesus shared with his followers. In it, he talks about God's commandments.

There are also many parallels to the Ten Commandments that can be found in Islam, the religion of Muslim people. The Koran, which is the holy book of Islam, commands that followers worship only one God. There are also laws against killing, bearing false witness, and adultery. And followers are commanded to honor their parents. These are all ideas found in the Ten Commandments.

The Koran

CHAPTER 11
The Commandments and the Founding Fathers

The Ten Commandments not only lay the groundwork for religions, they have left a mark on governments—for example, the government of the United States. After the Revolutionary War was won, a new country was born. The thirteen colonies of England suddenly became the United States of America. A constitution—a plan for how the government would work—had to be written. But it took time.

The war ended in 1783. There was no constitution ready at the end of the war to determine what the new country's laws would be. What rules were people supposed to follow? Benjamin Franklin, one of the country's founding fathers, said citizens would do well if they just lived by the Ten Commandments.

Of the fifty-five men at the constitutional convention of the United States, more than fifty were Christians. The men who wrote the Constitution used their knowledge of the commandments to shape the laws for the federal government and the states within the new country—like those forbidding murder and theft. But even though there is a strong relationship between some of the ideas found in the Ten Commandments and those found in the Constitution, the Constitution is not a religious document.

In the United States, there is no official government religion. Instead, all religions are to be respected and honored. People are allowed to choose the religion they want to follow. This was true when our country was established and it is true today.

Even so, religious ideas—especially the first commandment—do get represented. For example, our Pledge of Allegiance states:

I pledge allegiance to the flag of the United States of America and to the republic for which it stands, one nation, under God, indivisible, with liberty and justice for all.

By referring to one single God, this pledge

mirrors the very first commandment.

In addition, our national motto, "In God We Trust," also refers to the single God in the first commandment. "In God We Trust" first appeared on US coins in 1864 and has appeared on paper currency since 1957.

CHAPTER 12
The Ten Commandments Live On

The Ten Commandments have been depicted in art throughout the centuries. The famous Italian sculptor Michelangelo carved a marble statue of Moses.

Moses is seated and has a serious expression on his face. He holds the two tablets by his side. The tablets are still empty. The artist has chosen to show Moses at the moment right before he receives the commandments that will change his life and the lives of so many others. He seems to know that something very important is about to happen.

In a large oil painting by the Dutch artist Ferdinand Bol, Moses is shown coming down from Mount Sinai with the two tablets in his

arms. His followers kneel, or raise their arms in wonder. Angels with wings watch him as he goes.

Rembrandt, the famous seventeenth-century Dutch painter, painted Moses holding the tablets high above his head, ready to break and smash them. This refers to the Biblical story in which the Israelites return to worshipping idols, even after they have received the commandments. The artist captured Moses in this dramatic moment.

These are just a few examples. At different times and in different countries, artists have chosen to show Moses and the commandments in their work.

The Ten Commandments have also been the subject of several movies, two of which were made by the director Cecil B. DeMille. The first was a silent film made in 1923. The second was DeMille's last and most successful film. It was

made in 1956 and starred Charlton Heston as Moses, and Yul Brynner as Pharaoh. It was shot on location in Egypt, Mount Sinai, and the Sinai Peninsula and had one of the largest sets ever constructed for a film. At the time, it was the most expensive movie ever made.

In 1957, the film was nominated for seven Academy Awards including Best Picture. It won the Academy Award for Best Visual Effects. In 1998, Val Kilmer provided the voice of Moses in an animated feature film, *The Prince of Egypt*. Made in 2014, the movie *Exodus: Gods and Kings* starring Christian Bale and Joel Edgerton also told the story of Moses.

It is astonishing to think that a document written so many years ago can still have such an impact. The Ten Commandments have influenced history, religion, and culture. Their power will continue to be felt by people all over the world.

Timeline of the Ten Commandments

c. 1526 BC	Possible date for Moses's birth
c. 1504 BC	Hatshepsut becomes the second woman pharaoh
c. 1487 BC	Moses flees from Egypt
c. 1446 BC	Moses asks Pharaoh to let the Israelites go
	The Israelites escape from Egypt
	Moses receives the Ten Commandments on Mount Sinai
c. 1406 BC	Moses sees the Promised Land and dies
c. 1400 BC	The Israelites settle in the Promised Land
586 BC	Babylonians conquer Jerusalem, destroying the Temple of Solomon
515 BC	Construction completed on the Second Temple
c. AD 33	Death of Jesus
337	Roman emperor Constantine converts to Christianity

Timeline of the World

c. 1600 BC	Shang Dynasty founded in China
c. 1352 BC	Pharaoh Tutankhamen (King Tut) dies at about age nineteen
c. 1200 BC	Olmec civilization prospers in what is now Mexico
	Iron Age begins in East Africa
776 BC	First Olympic Games in Greece
c. 770 BC	Construction on the Great Wall of China begins
476 BC	The Great Wall of China is completed
438 BC	The Parthenon is completed in what is now Athens, Greece
332 BC	Alexander the Great conquers Egypt
51 BC	Cleopatra becomes queen of Egypt

Bibliography

*Books for young readers

*Bach, Alice, and Cheryl J. Exum. *Moses' Ark: Stories from the Bible.* New York: Delacorte Press, 1989.

*Hanft, Josh. *Miracles of the Bible.* Maplewood, NJ: Blue Apple, 2007.

*Hoffman, Mary. *Kings and Queens of the Bible.* New York: Henry Holt, 2008.

Segal, Lore. *The Book of Adam to Moses.* New York: Alfred A. Knopf, 1987.

*Tubb, Jonathan N. *Bible Lands.* New York: DK Eyewitness Books, 1991.

Dome of the Rock Islamic shrine on Temple Mount in Jerusalem, Israel

A poster for Cecil B. DeMille's 1956 movie *The Ten Commandments*

Michelangelo's marble statue of Moses

The plate used for Passover seder displays symbolic foods that commemorate the Exodus from Egypt.

A rabbi reads from the Torah in a synagogue.

GALI TIBBON/AFP/Getty Images

The largest replica of the Ark of the Covenant in Jerusalem

Rembrandt's painting of Moses with the Ten Commandments

A rabbi and his wife prepare for the evening Sabbath at home

Egyptian relief carving depicting scribes

Tourists exploring Mount Sinai in Egypt

Moſes zertrümmert die Geſetztafeln.

Als er aber nahe zum Lager kam und das Kalb und den Reigen ſahe, ergrimmete er mit Zorn, und warf die Tafeln aus ſeiner Hand und zerbrach ſie unten am Berge.
II Moſe. Cap. 32. v. 19.

A Joerdens.sc

Illustration of Moses breaking the commandment tablets

Statue of Egyptian god Anubis

The Ten Commandments

1 - I AM THE LORD THY GOD, THOU SHALT NOT HAVE STRANGE GODS BEFORE ME.

2 - THOU SHALT NOT TAKE THE NAME OF THE LORD THY GOD IN VAIN.

3 - REMEMBER THAT THOU KEEP HOLY THE SABBATH DAY.

Love God Above ALL

4 - HONOR THY FATHER AND THY MOTHER.

5 - THOU SHALT NOT KILL.

6 - THOU SHALT NOT COMMIT ADULTERY.

7 - THOU SHALT NOT STEAL.

8 - THOU SHALT NOT BEAR FALSE WITNESS AGAINST THY NEIGHBOR.

9 - THOU SHALT NOT COVET THY NEIGHBOR'S WIFE.

10 - THOU SHALT NOT COVET THY NEIGHBOR'S GOODS.

Love Thy Neighbor as Thyself

Ten Commandments tablets near the entryway of a church

Celebration of Passover seder

The Touro Synagogue in Newport, Rhode Island,
the oldest synagogue in America